The Story of the Civil Rights
MARCH ON WASHINGTON FOR JOBS AND FREEDOM
in Photographs

David Aretha

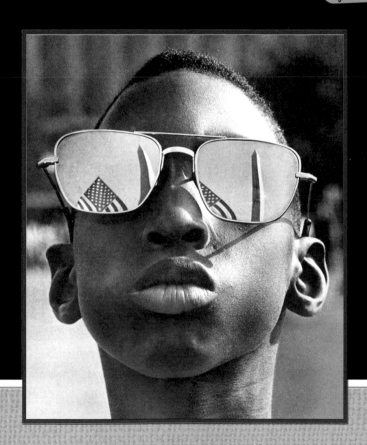

Enslow Publishers, Inc.
40 Industrial Road
Box 398
Berkeley Heights, NJ 07922
USA

http://www.enslow.com

Library of Congress Cataloging-in-Publication Data

Aretha, David.
    The story of the civil rights march on Washington for jobs and freedom in photographs / David Aretha.
        pages cm. — (The story of the civil rights movement in photographs)
    Includes index.
    Summary: "Discusses the March on Washington for Jobs and Freedom in 1963, including the causes for the march, how the march was organized and its leaders, the important speeches, and the impact it had on the Civil Rights Movement"—Provided by publisher.
    ISBN 978-0-7660-4238-4
    1. March on Washington for Jobs and Freedom (1963 : Washington, D.C.)—Juvenile literature. 2. March on Washington for Jobs and Freedom (1963 : Washington, D.C.)—Pictorial works. 3. Civil rights demonstrations—Washington (D.C.)—History—20th century—Juvenile literature. 4. Civil rights demonstrations—Washington (D.C.)—History—20th century—Pictorial works. 5. African Americans—Civil rights—History—20th century—Juvenile literature. 6. African Americans—Civil rights—History—20th century—Pictorial works. I. Title.
    F200.A74 2014
    975.3'041—dc23

                    2013004860

Future editions:
Paperback ISBN: 978-1-4644-0419-1   EPUB ISBN: 978-1-4645-1229-2
Singler-User PDF ISBN: 978-1-4646-1229-9   Multi-User PDF ISBN: 978-0-7660-5861-3

Printed in the United States of America
112013 Bang Printing, Brainerd, Minn.
10 9 8 7 6 5 4 3 2 1

To Our Readers: We have done our best to make sure all Internet Addresses in this book were active and appropriate when we went to press. However, the author and the publisher have no control over and assume no liability for the material available on those Internet sites or on other Web sites they may link to. Any comments or suggestions can be sent by e-mail to comments@enslow.com or to the address on the back cover.

♻ Enslow Publishers, Inc., is committed to printing our books on recycled paper. The paper in every book contains 10% to 30% post-consumer waste (PCW). The cover board on the outside of each book contains 100% PCW. Our goal is to do our part to help young people and the environment too!

Illustration Credits: AP Images, pp. 1, 2, 12, 13, 14, 16, 18, 20, 32 (bottom), 36, 39, 46 (top and bottom), 47; AP Images / Harry Harris, p. 8; Corbis Bettman / AP Images, p. 30; Library of Congress Prints and Photographs, pp. 3, 4, 10 (top and bottom), 24, 26, 34; National Archives and Records Administration, pp. 19, 22, 23, 28–29, 31, 32 (top), 40, 41, 42, 46 (middle).

Cover Illustration: AP Images: The top of the Washington Monument and part of a U.S. flag are reflected in the sunglasses of Austin Clinton Brown, 9, of Gainsville, Georgia.

Table of Contents

What Are Our Immediate Goals?

1. To mobilize five million Negroes into one militant mass for pressure.

2. To assemble in Chicago the last week in May, 1943, for the celebration of

"WE ARE AMERICANS – TOO" WEEK

And to ponder the question of Non-Violent Civil Disobedience and Non-Cooperation, and a Mass March On Washington.

WHY SHOULD WE MARCH?

15,000 Negroes Assembled at St. Louis, Missouri
20,000 Negroes Assembled at Chicago, Illinois
23,500 Negroes Assembled at New York City
Millions of Negro Americans all Over This Great Land Claim the Right to be Free!

FREE FROM WANT!
FREE FROM FEAR!
FREE FROM JIM CROW!

"Winning Democracy for the Negro is Winning the War for Democracy!" — A. Philip Randolph

440

This flyer shows that African Americans were staging large protest meetings as early as the 1940s.

Introduction

By 1941, more than seventy years had passed since slavery was abolished in the United States. But America's black citizens were not truly free, and A. Philip Randolph knew it. A longtime civil rights leader, Randolph was determined to make life better for his fellow African Americans. He once said that "the humblest and weakest person can enjoy the highest civil, economic, and social rights that the biggest and most powerful possess."

In the American South, segregation remained. A segregated society means that the dominant racial group separates and mistreats a less-powerful group. In the "Jim Crow" (segregated) South, white people held all the power. They completely controlled business, politics, the courts, and law enforcement. They passed laws that made it extremely difficult for black citizens to vote or get hired for well-paying jobs. African Americans were confined to separate and inferior facilities, including schools. They had to sit in the back of buses. They could use only "colored" drinking fountains and restrooms.

During the Great Depression in the 1930s, a sign in the South read: "No Jobs for [Blacks] Until Every White Man Has a Job." Outside of the South, America was not nearly as segregated. However, black students in non-southern states still attended subpar schools. African-American workers made far less money than white workers. Teaming with real estate agents, many white homeowners kept black citizens from moving into their neighborhoods.

In 1940, the economy was improving. America's allies—Great Britain and France—were fighting enemies in World War II. The United States was building weapons and vehicles to sell to France and Great Britain. Many Americans were getting jobs in the defense industry. But while American defense companies were hiring white workers at good salaries, they were not hiring many African Americans.

Randolph was a tall, eloquent civil rights leader. He preached that the U.S. government should eliminate racial discrimination when hiring defense-industry workers. In 1941, he and other civil rights leaders threatened a March on Washington to demand equal rights. Randolph once said: "Nothing counts but pressure, pressure, more pressure, and still more pressure through broad, organized, aggressive mass action."

Through Randolph's efforts, 100,000 African Americans were expected to show up in Washington, D.C., on July 1. President Franklin Roosevelt bowed to this pressure. On June 25, he issued an executive order to end racial discrimination in the defense industry, and he created the Fair Employment Practices Committee to monitor and enforce the order.

Randolph responded by canceling the March on Washington. However, as the years passed, he considered staging another march on the nation's capital. After all, black people's rights and lives were improving very little. In 1959, more than half of America's black citizens lived in poverty. In Mississippi in 1960, less than 7 percent of African Americans were registered to vote. In 1962, despite a 1954 U.S. Supreme Court decision outlawing racial segregation in public education, more than 99 percent of black students in the South went to black-only schools.

In 1962, Randolph suggested to friend Bayard Rustin another March on Washington. This march would focus on jobs. Randolph believed that conditions would improve for African Americans only if their employment status improved. At the time, the average black worker in the United States made about half as much money as the average white worker. A black laborer was about twice as likely to be unemployed.

Randolph wanted to stage an Emancipation March for Jobs on January 1, 1963. That date was the 100th anniversary of the Emancipation Proclamation. On January 1, 1863, during the Civil War, President Abraham Lincoln had proclaimed that the slaves in the southern rebelling states were free.

However, Randolph could not get support for the march from other civil rights leaders. At the time, many civil rights activists were focusing on getting black Southerners registered to vote. Others were involved in sit-ins. In a sit-in, for example, black activists would go to a whites-only restaurant and would not leave until they were served.

In the opening months of 1963, Martin Luther King, Jr., and fellow civil rights leaders began planning an assault on segregation in Birmingham, Alabama's largest city. That spring, they staged large protest marches on Birmingham's streets. King himself urged the city's black citizens to march. "In spite of the difficulties—and we are going to have a few more difficulties—keep climbing," he preached. "Keep moving. If you can't fly, run! If you can't run, walk! If you can't walk, crawl! But by all means keep moving."

Bull Connor, a strong supporter of segregation, was in charge of Birmingham's police and fire departments. When hundreds of young black activists marched on May 3, Connor ordered the police to go after them with attack dogs. He also ordered firefighters to blast them with powerful fire hoses.

Many Americans who witnessed these images on television were appalled. All across the land, people demanded an end to racial discrimination in the South. In a 1963 Gallup poll of U.S. citizens, civil rights was listed as the most important crisis facing America. President John F. Kennedy agreed. In 1963, he proposed a civil rights bill designed to end segregation.

King knew that it wouldn't be easy passing such a bill in Congress. The Senate and House of Representatives were comprised of many southern segregationists (those who supported segregation). As in previous years, they would strongly oppose such a bill.

King believed that a massive march on Washington would help get a strong civil rights bill passed. He wanted members of Congress to look up and see thousands of people demanding racial justice. According to Taylor Branch's book *Pillar of Fire*, King talked on the phone to colleague Stanley Levison. King said, "We are on a breakthrough." He said it was time for "a mass protest" . . . a "mass march" on Washington. They agreed that to "really push" civil rights legislation, they needed a march of "possibly a hundred thousand people."

King was eager to team with Randolph on this project. Though seventy-four years old, Randolph was excited by the challenge. That June, Randolph said directly to President Kennedy: "There *will* be a march!" And there was.

Chapter 1

Planning for
100,000

The "Big Six" were in charge of the March on Washington. They included (left to right) John Lewis, Whitney Young, A. Philip Randolph, Martin Luther King, Jr., James Farmer, Jr., and Roy Wilkins. All but Randolph headed a major civil rights organization.

Rustin Takes Charge

On July 2, 1963, fifteen civil rights leaders met in New York to plan the March on Washington for Jobs and Freedom. But for NAACP (National Association for the Advancement of Colored People) chief Roy Wilkins, fifteen leaders were too many. According to historian Taylor Branch in *Parting the Waters,* Wilkins "began literally to tap the men on the shoulders, saying 'This one stays. This one goes.'" In the end, six leaders remained.

Bayard Rustin, Randolph's longtime friend, was in charge of planning the event. Rustin had to organize a march for 100,000 people—and had less than two months to do it! The event would take place on August 28.

First, the organizing committee needed to raise funds, specifically $75,000. The NAACP, other organizations, and individuals donated money. Organizers also had to recruit people to come to the March. One newsletter stated: "In the South, plans are under way for a Freedom Train from Tallahassee, Florida on August 27, and will travel along the east coast to Washington, picking up people as it goes."

At the March site, organizers would install a giant green tent that would serve as March headquarters. Rustin also arranged for several thousand portable toilets, twenty-one drinking fountains, and dozens of doctors and nurses. Volunteers agreed to provide sandwiches, fruit, and drinks to marchers. Organizers also made thousands of signs, such as "We Demand Equal Rights Now."

The great event was coming together!

MARCH ON WASHINGTON FOR JOBS AND FREEDOM AUGUST 28, 1963

We Shall

Overcome

This flyer promotes the upcoming March on Washington. "We Shall Overcome" was the most popular of the "freedom songs," which were sung by civil rights activists.

This program lists the March's speakers and musical performers. Martin Luther King, Jr., would deliver the final "Remarks."

MARCH ON WASHINGTON FOR JOBS AND FREEDOM
AUGUST 28, 1963
LINCOLN MEMORIAL PROGRAM

1. The National Anthem
2. Invocation — Led by Marian Anderson.
   The Very Rev. Patrick O'Boyle, *Archbishop of Washington.*
3. Opening Remarks — A. Philip Randolph, *Director March on Washington for Jobs and Freedom.*
4. Remarks — Dr. Eugene Carson Blake, *Stated Clerk, United Presbyterian Church of the U.S.A.; Vice Chairman, Commission on Race Relations of the National Council of Churches of Christ in America.*
5. Tribute to Negro Women Fighters for Freedom — Mrs. Medgar Evers
   Daisy Bates
   Diane Nash Bevel
   Mrs. Medgar Evers
   Mrs. Herbert Lee
   Rosa Parks
   Gloria Richardson
6. Remarks
7. Remarks — John Lewis, *National Chairman, Student Nonviolent Coordinating Committee.*
8. Remarks — Walter Reuther, *President, United Automobile, Aerospace and Agricultural Implement Wokers of America, AFL-CIO; Chairman, Industrial Union Department, AFL-CIO.*
9. Selection — James Farmer, *National Director, Congress of Racial Equality.*
10. Prayer — Eva Jessye Choir
11. Remarks — Rabbi Uri Miller, *President Synagogue Council of America.*
12. Remarks — Whitney M. Young, Jr., *Executive Director, National Urban League.*
13. Remarks — Mathew Ahmann, *Executive Director, National Catholic Conference for Interracial Justice.*
14. Selection — Roy Wilkins, *Executive Secretary, National Association for the Advancement of Colored People.*
15. Remarks — Miss Mahalia Jackson
16. Remarks — Rabbi Joachim Prinz, *President American Jewish Congress.*
17. The Pledge — The Rev. Dr. Martin Luther King, Jr., *President, Southern Christian Leadership Conference.*
18. Benediction — A Philip Randolph
    Dr. Benjamin E. Mays, *President, Morehouse College.*

"WE SHALL OVERCOME"

Spreading Fear

The March organizers planned for a peaceful event. However, some Americans feared that the event could turn violent. Reported *Ebony* magazine in 1963: ". . . ripples of fear spread across the nation. Powerful politicians . . . urged the leaders to abandon the March. . . . The press took up the cry, saying with increasing stridence that the March was social dynamite and that violence was almost unavoidable."

Senator Olin D. Johnston of South Carolina said: "You should know that criminal, fanatical [people] will move in to take every advantage of this mob."

Event organizers were risking their lives. Every day for more than a week, bomb threats were made at the March headquarters in New York and Washington. But the organizers refused to be timid. As part of the event, they distributed a list of ten demands. Most importantly, they insisted that Congress pass "comprehensive and effective civil rights legislation." They demanded adequate education for black students, an end to segregation, and no more voting barriers.

At least President John F. Kennedy supported the cause. "I look forward to being here," he said. "I am sure members of Congress will be here. We want citizens to come to Washington if they feel that they are not having their rights expressed."

No Alcohol—Or Baseball

In the days before the March, excitement was building. Organizers started to think that perhaps 200,000 people would descend on Washington. "Freedom Buses" and "Freedom Trains" were coming from all over the country. But in the nation's capital, excitement was mixed with dread. Having witnessed the violence in Birmingham in May, the citizens of Washington feared the worst. For August 28, city officials banned the sale of alcohol to prevent drunken rowdiness. Taking precautions, the Washington Senators baseball team delayed two games.

Bayard Rustin was in charge of organizing the massive event. Rustin had been a leading civil rights activist since the 1940s. He had even been an adviser to Martin Luther King, Jr., during the famous Montgomery bus boycott in 1956.

Marchers would only be allowed to carry signs produced by the organizing committee. Committee leaders didn't want homemade, hateful signs to be part of the event.

Bring Sandwiches . . . But No Mayonnaise!

March organizers did all they could to keep visitors informed. Bayard Rustin handed out charts, schedules, and handbooks so that the event would take place in an orderly fashion. To keep marchers from going hungry, volunteers at New York's Riverside Church packed 80,000 bag lunches. Organizers told marchers to bring lots of water, wear comfortable shoes, and bring a raincoat just in case. They were told not to bring sandwiches with mayonnaise. In hot weather, mayonnaise could spoil and cause intestinal distress. And that would not be good!

Members of the Congress of Racial Equality (CORE) show their dedication to civil rights. Here, on August 15, they leave New York before dawn. They were about to begin a 230-mile walk to the March on Washington for Jobs and Freedom.

Chapter 2

The Road to
FREEDOM

All Aboard!

On August 27, 1963, civil rights supporters flocked to Washington, D.C. In Florida, a long "Freedom Special" train headed north. As it roared through Georgia, the Carolinas, and Virginia, freedom lovers climbed aboard. Trains, buses, and cars transported thousands of people to the nation's capital. On board, people sang and clapped. A train from Chicago even included a small jazz band. One senior citizen said he was not bothered by his twenty-four hour bus trip. "You forget," he told the *New York Times*, "we Negroes have been riding buses all our lives."

Roosevelt Nesmith of New Jersey shows the Washington Monument to his son, Roosevelt Noel, on August 27. They were among the many who would proudly say, decades later, "I was there."

On Bicycles and Roller Skates

A few days before the March, six people climbed into an old Ford automobile in Los Angeles, California. They were going to Washington, passenger David Parker said, "because my people got troubles."

All across America, citizens were headed to the March on Washington for Jobs and Freedom. Black Americans went because they wanted to show their support for civil rights. They were tired of being treated like second-class citizens. They were tired of working long, hard hours for little money. Moreover, black parents wanted their children to have opportunities that they didn't have. Many white citizens also supported the civil rights cause.

Most marchers came via train, bus, car, and airplane. But others used alternative forms of transportation. Jay Hardo, for example, rode his bicycle from Dayton, Ohio, to Washington. He was eighty-two years old! Ledger Smith roller-skated to the event . . . from Chicago. In Alabama, teenagers Robert Thomas, Robert Avery, and James F. Smith just started walking. They were fortunate to get a ride, and they wound up arriving several days early. With nothing to do, they helped the organizing committee.

Before the sun rose on August 28, vehicles poured in to Washington, D.C. "When [our] train pulled into Union Station," said Reverend Abraham Woods, "we saw buses coming from everywhere filled with people. I'm telling you, we were just elated."

Riders disembark from their buses on the morning of August 28. All told, approximately two thousand buses rolled into the city. Each bus had a "captain," who gave instructions to the passengers. Visitors were told to gather in front of the Washington Monument.

Swarming into Washington

Never before had so many people gathered in Washington, D.C. Teenager Ericka Jenkins, who lived in the nation's capital, headed to the Washington Monument. "I've never been so awestruck," she recalled. "They came every way—flatbed trucks with the wood floor that they used to carry tobacco, pickup trucks that were all dinged up, charter buses, school buses, station wagons, cars, motorcycles, bicycles, tricycles, and I could see people still coming in groups."

The Crowd Swells

By 9 A.M., approximately 40,000 people had gathered on the large, grassy area. By 11 A.M., the crowd had expanded to nearly 100,000. Organizers worried that the gathering was too big. Long lines formed at the drinking fountains and toilets. It was getting warmer, and the forecast called for a hot, humid day. Despite the concerns, most marchers were well-hydrated, well-fed, and content. Ambulances would send several dozen people to a hospital for heat exhaustion. However, only four of those people had to be admitted. No one died at the March.

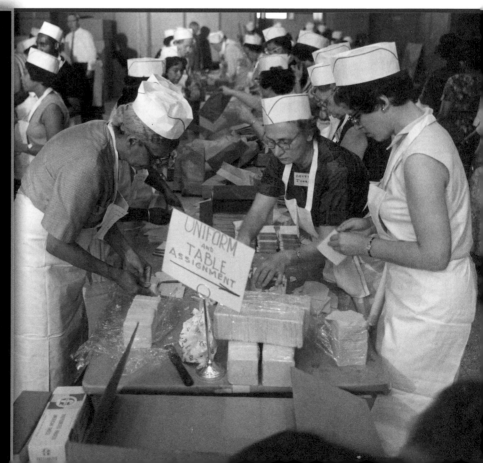

The organizing committee couldn't afford to hire service workers. Instead, they relied on an army of volunteers. Here, people make sandwiches to feed the masses. For 50 cents each, many people purchased cheese-sandwich bag lunches.

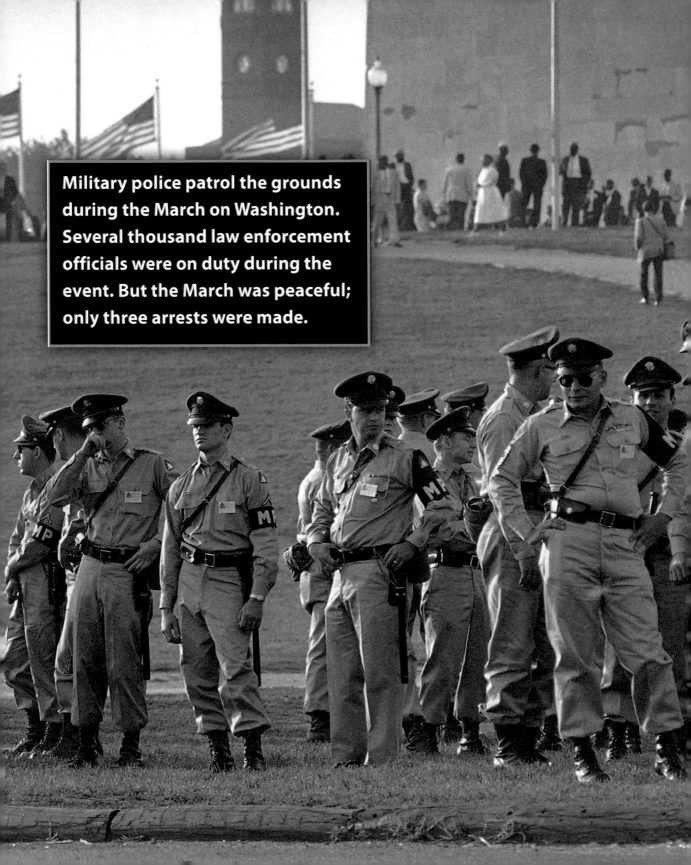

Military police patrol the grounds during the March on Washington. Several thousand law enforcement officials were on duty during the event. But the March was peaceful; only three arrests were made.

Chapter 3

Morning at the MARCH

An Act of Kindness

By late morning, the March on Washington had become the largest protest event ever in the nation's capital. People were also amazed to see blacks and whites joining together for the cause of equality. About one out of every four people at the event was white. One black woman was impressed by how nice the white demonstrators treated her: "Why, when I was out there at the March a white man stepped on my foot, and he said, 'Excuse me,' and I said 'Certainly! . . .' I believe that was the first time a white person has ever really been nice to me."

Folksingers Joan Baez and Bob Dylan performed at the event. Baez opened with "Oh Freedom." Later, she and Dylan sang "When the Ship Comes In."

Music in the Air

Beginning at 10 A.M., musical artists entertained the crowd near the Washington Monument. The trio of Peter, Paul & Mary sang their hit song "Blowin' in the Wind," which had been written by Bob Dylan. In the lyrics, Dylan asks how many years can people (African Americans) exist before they're allowed to be free. The answer, he says, is blowing in the wind.

Many Hollywood celebrities wanted to show their support for the cause. They included famous actors Sidney Poitier, Harry Belafonte, and Charlton Heston (left to right).

Police officers carry away a woman who likely was in need of medical attention.

Tension Builds

Though the crowd of 200,000 was orderly, the event went off course in late morning. At 11:30 A.M., the event's leaders were supposed to lead the crowd from the Washington Monument to the Lincoln Memorial. That's where the main program would be held. However, these leaders were still at the Capitol, where they were talking with members of Congress. Around that time, the marchers walked to the Lincoln Memorial by themselves. "They're *going*!" Rustin shouted from the Capitol. "We're supposed to be leading *them*!"

A bigger problem involved the speech of John Lewis, head of the Student Nonviolent Coordinating Committee (SNCC). Leaders of the event, as well as those in the Kennedy Administration, read the speech beforehand. They thought it was too "angry." At one point, Kennedy aide Burke Marshall arrived with revisions to the speech. Lewis did not want to make those changes.

In addition, Reverend Fred Shuttlesworth—a major civil rights leader from Birmingham, Alabama—was upset because he wanted to speak during the program. Also, the crowd was getting bigger, the temperature was rising, and humidity was setting in. Would the afternoon be a success or a disaster? By noon, no one could say for sure.

Chapter 4

Demanding JUSTICE

Televised from Coast to Coast

Shortly after 1 P.M., the main program was scheduled to begin in front of the Lincoln Memorial. Chairs were set up for members of Congress and other special guests. Most of the crowd would stand in a grassy, rectangular-shaped area. It stretched from the Lincoln Memorial to the Washington Monument, a distance of nearly one mile.

Meanwhile, CBS television covered the afternoon program live. Never before had civil rights been given so much TV exposure. For the first time, millions of Americans would hear Martin Luther King, Jr., deliver a speech. The words of all the speakers would have a profound impact on the nation.

Organizers had said the March would "be nonviolent, but not timid." That is how it played out. Marchers protested peacefully, but their signs demanded strong action immediately.

WE MARCH FOR JOBS FOR ALL NOW!
WE MARCH FOR JOBS FOR ALL NOW!
WE DEMAND VOTING RIGHTS NOW!
WE DEMAND
UAW SAYS: END SEGREGATED RULES IN PUBLIC SCHOOLS
WE MARCH FOR INTEGRATED SCHOOLS NOW!

In late morning, tens of thousands of demonstrators headed toward the Lincoln Memorial. The March leaders raced over to the crowd. They held hands (pictured) and made it appear as if they were leading them. In reality, thousands of people were already ahead of these men.

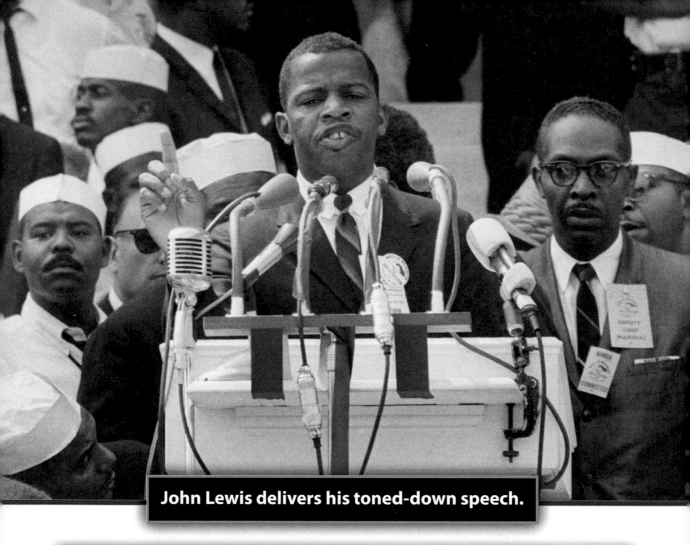

John Lewis delivers his toned-down speech.

"How Long Can We Be Patient?"

Shortly after 1:30, singer Marian Anderson began the program with the National Anthem. After remarks by A. Philip Randolph and others, John Lewis stepped to the podium. Just minutes earlier, Martin Luther King, Jr., had helped Lewis revise his speech. But it was still fiery. "We are tired of being beat by policemen," Lewis declared. "We are tired of seeing our people locked up in jail over and over again, and then you holler 'Be patient.' How long can we be patient? We want our freedom and we want it now."

A Long Afternoon

Over loudspeakers, more than a dozen civil rights and religious leaders addressed the gathering. Many speakers delivered strong messages. "It is simply incomprehensible . . ." said Roy Wilkins, "that the U.S. government—which can regulate the contents of a pill—apparently is powerless to prevent the physical abuse of citizens within its own borders." The speeches were well written, but perhaps there were too many of them. By midafternoon, those in the crowd appeared to be bored.

All told, at least 250,000 people attended the March on Washington. The crowd stretched from the Washington Monument (pictured) to the Lincoln Memorial.

Demonstrators sit on the Lincoln Memorial during the afternoon program. Many college students, black and white, supported the civil rights cause.

The Washington Monument and an American flag are reflected in the sunglasses of Austin Clinton Brown. The nine-year-old boy came all the way from Gainesville, Georgia, to attend the historic event.

Chapter 5

King's
DREAM

A Patient Crowd

To attend the March on Washington, most every person made sacrifices. They had traveled great distances to be there. They walked a couple miles or more throughout the day. They endured temperatures in the high 80s and stifling humidity. And they stood patiently through speech after speech. Archbishop Patrick O'Boyle, Rabbi Uri Miller, and National Urban League executive director Whitney Young were among the speakers that day. But those who endured were rewarded at the end. Gospel singer Mahalia Jackson excited the crowd, and Martin Luther King, Jr., gave them a moment they would never forget.

The luckiest demonstrators sat around the large Reflecting Pool. They not only got to sit down, but they cooled their tired feet. The scene was ironic. In the segregated South, many whites had never wanted to be in the same pools as blacks.

Words of Wisdom

Roy Wilkins, the head of the NAACP, was a mild-mannered man. Despite a well-worded speech, he didn't exactly excite the crowd. But the next person to step to the microphones, Mahalia Jackson, did. A gospel singer with a booming voice, Jackson stirred the gathering with "How I Got Over." With her face straining and body swaying, Jackson sang, "One day, I'm gonna join the heavenly choir! I'm gonna sing and never get tired!"

Jackson followed up with "I Been 'Buked and I Been Scorned." The crowd clapped and danced, and some even cried. For the next speaker, Rabbi Joachim Prinz, it was a tough act to follow. "I wish I could sing!" Prinz quipped. But the rabbi's speech was no laughing matter. He talked about his years in Germany, when Adolf Hitler's Nazi Party oppressed and killed Jewish people and others. The rest of the world did virtually nothing to stop them.

"When I was the rabbi of the Jewish community in Berlin under the Hitler regime, I learned many things," Prinz said. "The most important thing that I learned under those tragic circumstances was that bigotry and hatred are not the most urgent problem. The most urgent, the most disgraceful, the most shameful, and the most tragic problem is silence."

The lesson was clear: Americans had an obligation to help their fellow citizens.

Martin Luther King, Jr., declared: "We will not be satisfied until justice rolls down like waters, and righteousness like a mighty stream."

"I Have a Dream!"

After Rabbi Prinz spoke, A. Philip Randolph introduced the most anticipated speaker of the day: "I have the pleasure to present to you Dr. Martin Luther King, Jr.!"

King went on to deliver one of the most inspiring speeches in American history. He talked about black citizens who had been "battered by the storms of persecution and staggered by the winds of police brutality." He urged them not to "wallow in the valley of despair." At one point, Mahalia Jackson shouted, "Tell 'em about the dream, Martin!" And that's when the speech really picked up.

"I have a dream that one day on the red hills of Georgia, the sons of former slaves and the sons of former slave owners will be able to sit down together at the table of brotherhood," King bellowed. "I have a dream that one day even the state of Mississippi, a state sweltering with the heat of injustice, sweltering with the heat of oppression, will be transformed into an oasis of freedom and justice."

Looking upward and shaking his head, King declared: "I have a dream that my four little children will one day live in a nation where they will not be judged by the color of their skin but by the content of their character. I have a dream today!"

The crowd erupted in applause.

Chapter 6

A Day of
INSPIRATION

Cheers and Tears

Martin Luther King, Jr., concluded his speech amid a thunderous ovation. With his final words, he said he looked forward to the day when "we will be able to join hands and sing in the words of the old Negro spiritual: Free at last! Free at last! Thank God Almighty, we are free at last!"

"People hung on every word," said civil rights activist Eleanor Holmes Norton. "He preached slowly enough so that we could hear his words and savor them and see how wonderful they were." Freedom lovers in the crowd howled their approval and pumped their fists in the air. Many hugged one another, and some cried tears of joy.

Martin Luther King, Jr., acknowledges the crowd at the March on Washington. His friend, Clarence Jones, said that King's speech was so hot the words "were burning off the page!"

Marchers react to Martin Luther King, Jr.'s speech. King had brought the crowd to life after a long, hot, and humid afternoon.

A Huge Success

At 5 P.M., the March on Washington program ended on schedule. With King's words still ringing in their ears, many demonstrators walked with a skip in their step. The event, despite all the challenges, had been a huge success. Many gave credit to Bayard Rustin. "Rustin, I have to hand it to you," one of the leaders reportedly said. "You're a genius."

The President's Approval

After the program, the March on Washington leaders went to the White House. "I have a dream," Kennedy said with a smile to Martin Luther King, Jr. The leaders talked to the president for more than an hour. They urged him to help pass a strong civil rights bill. Afterward, Kennedy praised all of the people who had attended the March. "One cannot help but be impressed with the deep fervor and the quiet dignity that characterize the thousands who have gathered in the nation's capital," the president said.

President John F. Kennedy (center, light suit) meets with civil rights leaders immediately after the March on Washington. A. Philip Randolph stands to his right.

A girl hoists a March on Washington pennant that states, "I was there." At least 250,000 people (some reports say 300,000) could make that claim.

"An Unforgettable Demonstration"

After the March on Washington, demonstrators left the city without a major incident. Workers and volunteers began to clean up the area. The event had inspired most everyone, including politicians. "The heart of the American Negro was revealed today," U.S. Senator Jacob Javits stated. "This was an unforgettable demonstration. It was dignified, extraordinarily disciplined, and intensely patriotic."

Mahalia Jackson was overjoyed by the experience. "People were afraid before, but there's nothing to fear now," she was quoted as saying in the *Washington Post*. "I have high hopes that everything is going to come out all right."

Jackson may have been too optimistic. After all, segregation remained in much of the South. Adam Clayton Powell, a U.S. congressman and civil rights activist, said: "It was a great day for the civil rights movement, but we've got to have more of this type of thing before we are free."

Sadly, some demonstrators faced a rude awakening as they headed back home. As buses returned to the South, many riders were not served at "whites only" restaurants and rest stops. Outside of Meridian, Mississippi, angry segregationists roughed up some riders. On an expressway in Maryland, buses were pelted with rocks and rifle shots.

America still had a long way to go to fulfill the dream of Martin Luther King, Jr.

Conclusion

Watching on television, the March on Washington inspired millions of Americans. Many believed it marked a new beginning: Whites and blacks would work in harmony to create a better America. The civil rights song "A Change Is Gonna Come," recorded by Sam Cooke later in 1963, reflected that spirit.

But in the South, segregationists resisted such changes. Three weeks after the March, a terrible tragedy occurred in Birmingham, Alabama. On a Sunday morning, a bomb exploded at the Sixteenth Street Baptist Church. Four young African-American girls were killed.

That incident angered Americans of all colors. In New York City, protesters raised a sign that read "Arrest Wallace Now." It referred to Alabama governor George Wallace, a famous segregationist. Then, on November 22, 1963, President Kennedy was assassinated. Many wondered what would happen to Kennedy's proposed civil rights bill. Would it be set aside and never passed?

Another president may have let that happen. But not Kennedy's successor, Lyndon Johnson. President Johnson was one of the few white southern politicians who strongly supported civil rights. Johnson urged Congress to work with him to help continue Kennedy's policies. He stated that "no memorial, oration or eulogy could more eloquently honor President Kennedy's memory than the earliest possible passage of the civil rights bill for which he fought so long."

Southern politicians strongly opposed the bill, but it passed anyway. On July 2, 1964, President Johnson signed the civil rights bill into law. Appropriately, he handed one of the signing pens to Martin Luther King, Jr.

This Civil Rights Act of 1964 banned discrimination in public facilities. It also gave the U.S. attorney general more power to file lawsuits in order to protect citizens against discrimination. And it established the Equal Employment Opportunity Commission, which would strive to prevent discrimination in workplaces.

After the Civil Rights Act, segregation diminished greatly in the South. Business owners began taking down their "Colored" and "Whites Only" signs. Black citizens could sit where they wanted to on buses. They could eat in restaurants of their choice. Pools, beaches, libraries, parks, and movie theaters became integrated.

In 1965, Congress passed the Voting Rights Act. Afterward, African Americans began to vote in large numbers. They elected mayors, Congress members, and other politicians who were sensitive to their needs.

Unfortunately, African Americans have not yet achieved true equality. Even today, black workers make far less money than whites. About one-quarter of black citizens live in poverty, compared to less than 10 percent of white people. Most black children grow up in crowded cities, not the suburbs, and many attend below-average schools. It is hard to advance in life when you don't have much money or a good education.

Nevertheless, African Americans enjoy freedoms today that they only dreamed about prior to 1963. Increasingly, they are judged "not by the color of their skin, but by the content of their character."

In that regard, Martin Luther King, Jr.'s dream has been fulfilled.

1865–1965: After slavery, African Americans in the South are confined to segregated (separate, inferior) facilities. They are denied citizenship rights, such as voting.

1954: The U.S. Supreme Court bans segregation in public schools.

1955–1956: Martin Luther King, Jr., leads a successful yearlong boycott of segregated buses in Montgomery, Alabama.

1957: The National Guard helps black students integrate Central High School in Little Rock, Arkansas.

1960–mid-1960s: Civil rights activists stage hundreds of sit-ins at segregated restaurants, stores, theaters, libraries, and many other establishments.

1961: Activists stage Freedom Rides on segregated buses in the South.

1963: Thousands of African Americans protest segregation in Birmingham, Alabama.

1963: A quarter million Americans attend the March on Washington for Jobs and Freedom.

1964: Activists register black voters in Mississippi during "Freedom Summer."

1964: The U.S. Congress passes the Civil Rights Act. It outlaws segregation and other racial injustices.

1965: African Americans protest voting injustice in Selma, Alabama.

1965: Congress passes the Voting Rights Act, which guarantees voting rights for all Americans.

Further Reading

Books

Brimner, Larry Dane. *We Are One: The Story of Bayard Rustin.* Honesdale, Pa.: Calkins Creek, 2007.

Doak, Robin S. *The March on Washington: Uniting Against Racism.* Minneapolis, Minn.: Compass Point Books, 2008.

Ingram, Scott. *The 1963 Civil Rights March.* Milwaukee, Wis.: World Almanac Library, 2005.

Jones, Clarence and Stuart Connelly. *Behind the Dream: The Making of the Speech That Transformed a Nation.* New York: Palgrave MacMillan, 2011.

Internet Addresses

History.com: Civil Rights Movement
<http://www.history.com/topics/civil-rights-movement>

The March on Washington for Jobs and Freedom
<http://www.pbs.org/newshour/extra/2003/08/the-march-on-washington-for-jobs-and-freedom/>

Index